The American Dream Around the Dinner Table Religion and Politics II

Charles A Banks

Charles and Stephanie Banks

Printed in the United States of America

First Printing, 2015
Second Printing, 2019 2nd Edition

To my darling wife Stephanie and children; Chelsey (Archie), Peyton, Katarina, and grandbaby O with love. Thank you for believing in me on my quest towards writing a book that comes directly from my heart and soul.

To my in laws: Mike and Sharon Shanahan, thanks for always being there for us in our most difficult of times, we love you so much.

To my mother Sally Banks, thank you for believing in me and for your upbringing you have bestowed upon me.

To my late father Gerald Banks, you are truly my best friend, thank you, you have had a direct impact on my life every step of the way and continue to provide me strength and insight. See you again, later on down the road.

About the Author

Charles Banks was born in a small rural Iowa town in 1972. Charles owes everything to his great parents Gerald and Sally Banks. Charles Banks is the father of three wonderful children: Chelsey (Donald), Peyton, and Katarina and grandfather of Orion Joseph. Charles has been married for over 20 years to the love of his life Stephanie Banks Charles and Stephanie are both educators. Charles has been teaching for 16 years and has coached various sports.

Prior to Charles' educational experience, he worked in the Industrial sector as a Manager. Charles graduated from Graceland University in 2004 with a BA in History and Secondary Education and has graduated from Grand Canyon University with two Masters degrees; MA in Secondary Education and an MA in Education Administration. Charles is currently working on his PHD in Educational Leadership. Charles' life has been one of learning. Constantly searching for the truth. He was raised an Episcopalian and was later baptized within the Protestant faith. Charles believes in God, and loves his country.

Also, by Charles A. Banks

Paranormal Experiences: Death the Final Frontier. (2014)

Experiences From Beyond: Death the Final Frontier II. (2015)

Out of the Darkness and Into the Light: Death the Final Frontier III.   (2016)

Around the Dinner Table: Religion and Politics (The Butt Hurt Saga)(2016)

The Midwest Paranormal Road Trip (2017)

Death The Saga (2018)

Peering Into The Void (2018)

Contents

Dedicated to: my best friend Gerald Banks.

My dad was a special breed of soul. He loved, he lectured, he yelled, he showed compassion, he led by example, he was honest, and he was always around interested in how his family was doing at all times. I think I do a great job always being there for my children and family, but the idea of becoming the man, the myth, and the legend that my dad was is an entirely different perspective. He was my dad, my role model, my agent, and my best friend.

And to you the love of my life; Stephanie.

Acknowledgments

To my friends and colleagues: Kenny Attison, Candy Orton, Katrina the Good, and George Turner for helping me achieve my dream of writing and for truly understanding what I am trying to convey and believing in me. I am truly grateful.
I cannot express my full gratitude to all that was involved throughout the process of the book. Thanks to God, my in laws; Mike and Sharon Shanahan, my children, and grandbaby, and mother Sally Banks for sharing their experiences within the book. I would be remised if I did not mention the two

great women in my life; wife Stephanie and mother Sally, thank you so much for being in my life forever more. And to my Dad; see you on the other side.

 "Do you want to know who you are? Don't ask. Act! Action will delineate and define you."

- Thomas Jefferson

Foreword

Whether or not Albert Einstein quoted a statement regarding technology and the dumbing down of human interaction is not entirely conducive to our current situation in the world today. There were many factors throughout history that represent a world gone mad or a world that continues to compound information in a way that one becomes amassed in technology.

"I fear the day that technology will surpass our human interaction. The world will have a generation of idiots." **-Albert Einstein**

After researching this quote, I could not find it conclusive, or unsaid by Albert Einstein, so I am leaving the statement as it is. Human interaction is changing at an alarming rate. No longer are we sitting around the dinner table each night and discussing our lives in earnest. No longer are we conclusively living a life that our forefathers have lived. We live in a world of bitching and complaining and an unordered chaos is developing. As a society the United States is faltering in much the same way that the Roman Empire did in its demise to history. Much like 1968, the United States is at a crossroads in its development. The election of 2016 much like the election of 1968 will have many peaks and valleys and ultimately could cause a financial catastrophe or financial improvements brought on by a plutocracy that decides they cannot live without a middle or working class. We are at a crossroads.

Donald Trump, Hillary Clinton, Bernie Sanders, Jeb Bush, Ben Carson, Chris Christie, Ted Cruz, Carly Fiorina, Martin O'Malley, George Pataki, Rand Paul , Rick Santorum, Bobby Jindal, and Marco Rubio are all contenders for a job of a lifetime, which could seal our fate as a country. I placed these candidates in no uncertain order of Democrats or Republicans, because one thing remains irrevocably clear, they are vying to lead our great nation and they are all Americans. What I find interesting and funny is that the mere bringing up of one of these names at any establishment at any time may lead to what I would call the "butt hurt syndrome". Politics, religion, social gospel, and other factors that are applied to us via social media, internet, or on television play a key role in keeping the American people at each other's throats to avoid a clash where American's would rise up and take their country back from the establishment. Deep rhetoric to say the least, but true in my opinion, we have to educate ourselves and rise up or the American Dream will die forevermore.

Have you ever sat around the dinner table discussing religion and politics? If you grew up in my family you tended to just eat your food, discuss how your day went, and then be excused from the table. There was the occasional, you are going to vote for this guy or that guy is an idiot in my house, but there really were no deep descriptions of politics in general, unless my grandmother was present. I remember my father implying that I should never go to the dark side as he called them. As with any teenager, I tended to do the opposite of what their parent implied.

This book will explore personal experiences and experiences from dinner tables across the country. We will also look at the years from 1962-2015, which I contemplate as the years our freedoms died. Plausible deniability from our government regarding matters of Constitutional rights, which were guaranteed from our founding fathers, will be explored. Should we as a nation, sit idly by as our government continues to garnish our freedoms? What will you do if and when the economy crashes? Is there a reason why we have internment camps set up by the government that was created to protect its citizens? These are a few of the questions that I explore throughout the pages in the book. This will be a true testament to the will of our country, which is utterly protected by the First Amendment to the Constitution.

Together we will have a better understanding of where our country is headed and where we came from as a society. I question how many families do sit down and eat and congregate together each evening in their homes, the data would probably be staggering to say the very least.

If you were to walk into virtually any establishment around the country, you might see several men and women drinking coffee and discussing politics. If you were to walk into a home in the evening from the time period of 6:00-7:00 p.m. would you see a similar situation?

Chapter One: The Plutocracy that is America

One aspect that truly disgusts me as an American is the bipartisan commitment of our lawmakers and government. The ability to run the country through the eyes of the people is possible if lawmakers weren't entrenched in interest groups that sway leadership. Seemingly it seems our country is consistently headed towards a Plutocracy. A government based on the philosophy, which is implied as ruled by and for the rich.

There are numerous instances of elected officials being elected only to retire as multi-millionaires. Is this truly what is best for our country? Many live paychecks to pay check and others scratch and claw to make a living. However how many Americans are helping those in poverty? How many of us sit down at night and watch the TV and think about those struggling to make a living or the children in America starving? My guess is that virtually none of us think about the plethora of issues that our nation faces each and every day.

The main issue at fault here in my opinion starts with the grass roots movement within each of our congressional districts. Most people want to pay less tax, take care of people who need it, and live the American Dream. Whether you are a Democrat, Republican, or Independent we all want what is best for our country, which is to succeed. Why is it that so many in our government stipulate that they want what is best for the American people, but seemingly fall into the bipartisan debates? My guess is that the political system is flawed beyond repair.

Even more alarming is how the American people seem to accept the state our country and where it is headed, when there are issues many of us yammer about how the bad things are within our government. Yet we don't stand up to the government utilizing our Democratic prow less as stated within the constitution. Many don't even vote during elections because they feel they won't make a difference.

Imagine George Washington skipping the Constitutional Convention because he felt he wouldn't make a difference. Imagine if President Barak Obama didn't help with the inner-city people in need because he felt it wouldn't have made a difference. Now this may seem a little beyond common since, however this is what many of us do each and every day. Conceding our rights and responsibilities because we feel we do not matter.

Plutocracy is a term that many in Washington D.C. and in state and local governments understand, but maybe not as well as you rationalize. There are three definitions of the term Plutocracy:

- "The rule or power of wealth or of the wealthy."

- "A government or state in which the wealthy class rules.
- A class or group ruling, or exercising power or influence, by virtue of its wealth" (Dictionary, n.d).

The definition itself should make us as citizens apprehensive regarding where our country is headed.

Remarkably I am not the only individual that views our government and their intentions on the American people.

> *"In America today, the views of the voting public are nearly meaningless; wealthy individuals and business-backed special interest groups are almost entirely responsible for the stances that politicians take on the issues. That's the takeaway from a new study by Martin Gilens of Princeton University and Benjamin Page of Northwestern University"* (Light, 2014).

Imagine a country, which has no interest in their people, gaining ground from wealthy entities, and keeping this power from the American people.

Now look to past history, England for example. The barons passed the Magna Carta to garner more power from them in order to keep the king in check. This worked but for a short time. As the king and the barons fought for power, the normal workingman was left on the way side of political development. Then came the "The Petition of Right" the Petition of Right limited the monarch's authority and elevated the power of Parliament while extending the rights of the individual. As the country was in turmoil or as many people within the aristocracy would state, "the natives are restless", change was needed in order to establish a state that would run more efficiently in the eyes of the common man. At this point in English history, the power was taken not entirely from the king, but was made fair in many regards. The "Petition of Right" required the king to follow the law and gave certain rights to the common man.

The king could not imprison political critics without:

- Trial by jury
- Not declare martial law
- Rule by military during peacetime
- Require people to shelter troops without the homeowner's consent.

The main issue with the "Petition of Right" was that it had too many loopholes, which allowed the king to perpetuate certain powers if a crisis would arise.

Another key document within England's development that granted the rights of the individual was the "The English Bill of Rights (1689)" the Bill of Rights redefined the rights of Parliament and the rights of individuals.

- Prohibited a standing army in peacetime except with the consent of Parliament.
- Required that all parliamentary elections be free.
- Right to a fair and speedy trial.
- Freedom from excessive bail.
- Freedom from cruel and unusual punishment.

Much in American government and politics today is based on these early English ideas.

As I mentioned earlier, American's today often feel helpless, like they don't matter in the grand scheme of things. Imagine a country without Constitutional principles for our children, grandchildren, and everyday people within American democracy.

> "**We the People** of the United States, in Order to form a more perfect Union, establish Justice, insure domestic Tranquility, provide for the common defense, promote the general Welfare, and secure the Blessings of Liberty to ourselves and our Posterity, do ordain and establish this Constitution for the United States of America" (Constitution online, n.d).

"Blessings of Liberty to ourselves and our Posterity", these are words that the wealthy in our country need to hear. This does not state, ruled by the rich for the rich as would arise in a Plutocracy.

So, what can we do? Many of us certainly feel helpless, experience heart ache, and feel there is no place to turn. With that said, we need to exercise our freedoms as prescribed by the Constitution. Use the power that we all have as citizens of the United States. Stand up for your rights and values. We can do this by voting, getting involved in campaigns, writing our legislators, emailing our executives at the state and federal level, and volunteering our time. This power can't be taken away from us if we are willing to stand up to the Plutocracy that currently rules our Democracy. My ultimate goal would be that every American is well read with what is going on in our country. This will help circumvent the ploys of the wealthy elitists within our aristocracy and their plans to rule the country for their means only.

Chapter Two: Silver Spoon America

Recently during a classroom discussion regarding minimum wage and pay classification in the work place, I came to the realization that our world is heading toward a handout democracy. A handout democracy in my assessment is a society based on "WIFM", What's In it For Me. Ever contemplated that many of our lower socioeconomic class citizens feel as if they are undervalued, underpaid, and under respected? I would say this happens more than we realize.

Politics in general is a belated topic and is filled with certain dogma regarding the processes therein. With the lower socioeconomic classes rising

within our nation's population year
after fiscal year, we are constantly
promoting instability in the working
class. Is the Plutocracy that is
running our government mapping out the
doom of both the middle- and lower-
class structures in America? This is
difficult to understand; however, many
assume that the government wants
poverty to continue in order to
substantiate the wealthiest citizens
initiatives. I call on those that are
running in the 2016 election to answer
these questions.

What are your thoughts and
opinions regarding the minimum wage in
our country today? Have you ever
really thought about that living
paycheck to pay check scraping enough
money to pay utilities, rent, and just

enough money to put gas in the vehicle to get to work? Just this past week I passed a man leaving a convenience store after paying for gas. He obviously worked hard, his clothes were filthy, I assume he had just clocked out of an industrial job in the area. His facial expressions really rocked me to the core. No smile, a slumped over walk, a deep depressive look exhumed his moral fiber. I being the good-natured guy that I am said, "Hi" I was left with no reply. The man only looked forward got in his late 1970's rusty pick-up truck and left the area.

What strikes me immediately is how far we have declined in our moral fiber in our great country. Not for the man's resonating behavior or being ignored, but that we as a people accept those running our country right, wrong, or indifferent. That we would let our people fall from grace in such a manner decries what our nation's moral fabric has become. As a society, we have failed to become educated as to what the governments intentions are, regarding its people that it was intended to defend. We should all cry out from the banks across the nation as to the failure that our government has become. We should use out rights as citizens and vote, become active, and ultimately preserving our constitutional rights.

Anyway, enough with my soapbox and back to the task at hand, minimum wage. Should we raise it, or should we leave it alone? This is really a two-headed monster in my opinion. First, I will attempt to describe that of the working class. This can be divided up into several categories. I will break this up into three categories, I am sure that economists might change the vocabulary or strategies, but this makes since to me.

- Minimum wage earner
- Non-Full-time wage earner
- Full time employee

I will examine each of the three categories in depth through both personal and individual stories.

The year was 2001, our country was still reeling from the September 11th terrorist attacks, and our economy was falling at an incredible rate. During 2001, I was laid off from two jobs. The first job, a Plant Superintendent position in southern Iowa and the

second as a laborer position within a
steel foundry in the area. Both
positions paid very well in my opinion,
especially within the area I resided.
I was unemployed for the first time in
my life.

During my unemployment, I decided
to go back and finish my education. I
enrolled in Graceland University in
Lamoni, Iowa. My wife and I spent many
days discussing what I should do with
my life, I had always wanted to coach
football, and this would be a way to
obtain this goal in my life. I drove
75 miles one way to and from school on
a daily basis, which was very expensive
as gas prices rose due to the crisis in
September.

When my unemployment ran out, I
took a job with a fast food restaurant

in my hometown to help pay for the
necessities in our household. My wife
had a good job, wasn't full time but
paid pretty well in our area. Together
we made around $9,000.00 that year.
The year's prior I was averaging close
to $50,000.00. We lost our house and
our lively hood. Things were very
tight, we had no extras but the future
looked good due to the job market
within education. I believe minimum
wage during this time period was $7.00
per hour. I believe I worked on
average about 25 hours a week, way less
than was needed to make the trip on a
daily basis to Lamoni. Without the
help of both our parents, we would have
had a hard time reaching our goal
through graduation. To make matters
even worse financially, my wife became
pregnant about a year prior to

graduation. This would be the worst
financial strife that would hit my
family, however we were blessed with
our third child Katarina that same
year.

We struggled during these
tumultuous times and I graduated in the
spring of 2004. Just a few months
later in August we welcomed my youngest
daughter into the world. One month
prior to my daughter's birth, I was
offered a job as a teacher and as a
coach in my hometown, which I quickly
took. That school year I signed a
contract that would pay me $29,000.00.
Things were still tight, but we made it
through. Without an education I
believe that I wouldn't have been able
to make it out of the rut we were in.

This however wouldn't come cheap, as student loans began to pile up.

After a few years of raises in the school district my wife also became employed within the school. Things were starting to turn a corner for our family. Two years later my wife lost her job due to cuts made within the school district. This was due to Governor Terry Branstad's zero allowable growth initiative. We struggled again and again. Even making a good living currently, we continue to struggle. When will it end? Only God knows the answer regarding that question.

In class a student stated, "We should raise minimum wage to $15.00." I immediately thought back to all of the scratching and clawing that we faced with during differing time periods throughout my families lives. I brought up a valid point regarding hypothetically what would happen if the minimum wage were to be raised. Prices of everything would go up, businesses would feel the pinch, and taxes would rise. Am I right to assume this would be the case?

Minimum Wage Earner

A person that is expected to work up to 39 hours a week and most of the time would not be considered full time. Let's take a moment and put us in the shoes of those making minimum wage. Imagine paying your current bills, food, gas, clothing, and other bills you may have. We couldn't even fathom such a dire straight situation.

Now imagine a person making $100,000.00. You are living life to the fullest, your refrigerator is always full, you can eat out when you want, and you have all of your bills paid and a nest egg saved up. You lose your job. You are forced to use your nest egg even with your unemployment. Things get so tough you begin selling your cars and other items that you don't necessarily need. Your bills continue to pile up with no job with the same requirements in sight. You have to take out your 401K or other retirement. The money is really starting to dwindle at this point. Your children and spouse are starting to feel the pinch of the moment.

You get offered to take a job with a factory in your local area that pays minimum wage. Your unemployment is close to running out and the job pays only 1/3 what you made before you lost your job. What would you do? Does your opinion of government programs change? If the state and federal government were debating raising the minimum wage would you fret like you did when you were in a situation when you had your nest egg?

My guess is with any issue politically related is that we would continue to confine our beliefs within our political psyche until; we experienced certain situations that would change our moralistic makeup.

Full Time Employee

One that works at least 40 hours per week and garners benefits from their employers. Pay fluctuates depending on the particular industry that you are employed within. Currently I am in my 13th year within education and only now am earning what I was making back in 2001. 14 years after our drastic fall into poverty, we are starting to make the money that we were used to. We have a nice car, cable TV, cell phones, and a gorgeous home that we currently reside.

As we climbed back up into the lower middle class, we see things from a different perspective. We are blessed in many ways. The issue at hand here is that we are making the same wage that we were 14 years prior. This is an example of stagflation in my opinion. Stagflation is defined as a period where the prices of goods

increase and the wages stay the same.
Although we are making a good living,
we only have one car; we don't have
extras, and are only to put back a
small amount of money. One would
ponder why this is the case? For many
Americans, in order to get good jobs,
you have to be educated.

Like many, I am in debt out of my
eyeballs so to say in student loan
debt. We face the constant pressure of
paying our bills. My wife states on
many occasions, if she would have known
she would have had this hard a time
finding a job within education, she
wouldn't have gone back to school. I
agree with her assessment
wholeheartedly. Is this an example of
a handout type of society? Or is the
American Dream really dead? I will let

the reader decide these questions. I
can say that I feel beyond a shadow of
a doubt, that the more we are concerned
about getting by so to speak, the more
we are disenfranchised from the
political system.

As an individual on the outside
looking in, I can visualize that many
of our lawmakers take for granted
normal every day American citizens. I
state this because I have seen poverty,
I have experienced economic distress,
and I have seen many in governmental
positions make decisions that cause
real distress.

In 2008 Governor Terry Branstad
gave education a zero percent allowable
growth rate. School districts across
Iowa felt the pinch, cutting programs,

teachers, and needed technology. You could say that I am a little biased. This is true. My wife's job was cut due to the cut backs that were required in order for school districts to stay afloat. I used my democratic rights and contacted my state representatives. My representative did the best he could but didn't seem to gain ground due to bipartisan issues surrounding our state government.

Although we feel like our voices are not heard in our government, we need to use our power at each election that takes place. No matter your party affiliation, we must use our voting rights. Sadly, many don't take the opportunity to use their voting power. 2012 58.2% registered voters voted in 2008 61.6% (McDonald, 2013). From the

Presidential Turnout Rates chart, we can gather that interest in elections has increased from the lowest in 1996. There is still a need to get more eligible voters doing their part to share their voices in our democracy.

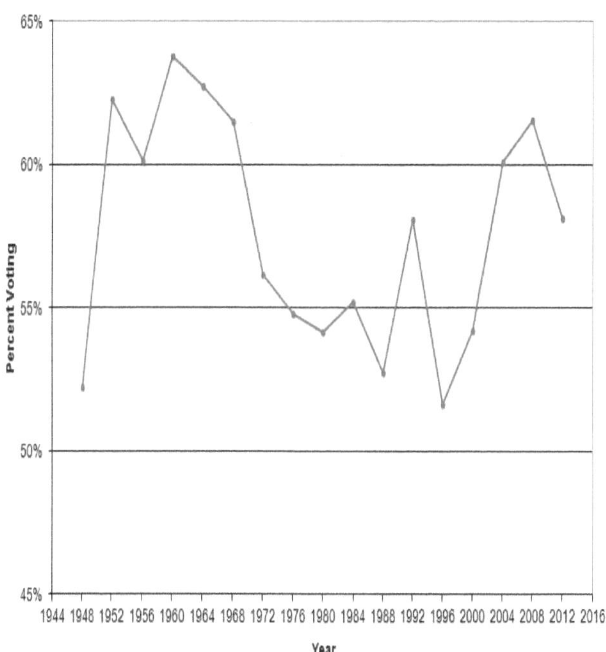

Chart from: (McDonald, 2013)

Silver Spoon America, in many regards is a term used to describe the state of which America has become. Instead of doing for others, we are constantly expecting others to do for us. The WIFM at its truest form. President Kennedy was an eloquent poet of what could happen had many within the aristocracy listened. One of the greatest speeches of all time in my opinion of a President that called on the nation to help one another for the sake of the nation, not for the sake of themselves.

John F. Kennedy's Inaugural Address, January 20, 1961

We observe today not a victory of party, but a celebration of freedom — symbolizing an end, as well as a beginning — signifying renewal, as well as change. For I have sworn before you and Almighty God the same solemn oath our forebears prescribed nearly a century and three quarters ago.

The world is very different now. For man holds in his mortal hands the power to abolish all forms of human poverty and all forms of human life. And yet the same revolutionary beliefs for which our forebears fought are still at issue around the globe — the belief that the rights of man come not from the generosity of the state, but from the hand of God.

We dare not forget today that we are the heirs of that first revolution. Let the word go forth from this time and place, to friend and foe alike, that the torch has been passed to a new generation of Americans — born in this century, tempered by war, disciplined by a hard and bitter peace, proud of our ancient heritage — and unwilling to witness or permit the slow undoing of those human rights to which this Nation has always been committed, and to which we are committed today at home and around the world.

Let every nation know, whether it wishes us well or ill, that we shall pay any price, bear any burden, meet any hardship, support any friend, oppose any foe, in order to assure the survival and the success of liberty.

This much we pledge — and more.

To those old allies whose cultural and spiritual origins we share, we pledge the loyalty of faithful friends. United, there is little we cannot do in a host of cooperative ventures. Divided, there is little we can do — for we dare not meet a powerful challenge at odds and split asunder.

To those new States whom we welcome to the ranks of the free, we pledge our word that one form of colonial control shall not have passed away merely to be replaced by a far more iron tyranny. We shall not always expect to find them supporting our view. But we shall always hope to find them strongly supporting their own freedom — and to remember that, in the past, those who foolishly sought power by riding the back of the tiger ended up inside.

To those peoples in the huts and villages across the globe struggling to break the bonds of mass misery, we pledge our best efforts to help them help themselves, for whatever period is required — not because the Communists may be doing it, not because we seek their votes, but because it is right. If a free society cannot help the many who are poor, it cannot save the few who are rich.

Let's take for a moment the statement; *"If a free society cannot help the many who are poor, it cannot save the few who are rich."* This is a daunting statement within my opinion. Why wouldn't we say we are trying to save all? Why do we need to implore a statement regarding the rich? Whether or not we are rich or not is not a question to rationalize. We should solemnly swear to save all American citizens and those throughout the world

that need our help from tyranny. This
is not a beginning of Plutocracy, but
it could for all practical purposes be
a push within that direction.

> *To our sister republics south of*
> *our border, we offer a special*
> *pledge — to convert our good words*
> *into good deeds — in a new*
> *alliance for progress — to assist*
> *free men and free governments in*
> *casting off the chains of poverty.*
> *But this peaceful revolution of*
> *hope cannot become the prey of*
> *hostile powers. Let all our*
> *neighbors know that we shall join*
> *with them to oppose aggression or*
> *subversion anywhere in the*
> *Americas. And let every other*
> *power know that this Hemisphere*
> *intends to remain the master of*
> *its own house.*

> *To that world assembly of*
> *sovereign states, the United*
> *Nations, our last best hope in an*
> *age where the instruments of war*
> *have far outpaced the instruments*
> *of peace, we renew our pledge of*

support — to prevent it from becoming merely a forum for invective — to strengthen its shield of the new and the weak — and to enlarge the area in which its writ may run.

Finally, to those nations who would make themselves our adversary, we offer not a pledge but a request: that both sides begin anew the quest for peace, before the dark powers of destruction unleashed by science engulf all humanity in planned or accidental self-destruction.

We dare not tempt them with weakness. For only when our arms are sufficient beyond doubt can we be certain beyond doubt that they will never be employed.

But neither can two great and powerful groups of nations take comfort from our present course — both sides overburdened by the cost of modern weapons, both rightly alarmed by the steady spread of the deadly atom, yet both racing to alter that

uncertain balance of terror that
stays the hand of mankind's final
war.

So, let us begin anew —
remembering   on both sides that
civility is not   a sign of weakness,
and sincerity is always subject to
proof. Let us   never negotiate out of
fear. But   let us never fear to
negotiate.

Let both sides explore what
problems unite us instead of
belaboring those problems which
divide us.

Let both sides, for the first
time, formulate serious and
precise proposals for the
inspection and control of arms —
and bring the absolute power to
destroy other nations under the
absolute control of all nations.

Let both sides seek to invoke the
wonders of science instead of its
terrors. Together let us explore
the stars, conquer the deserts,
eradicate disease, tap the ocean

depths, and encourage the arts and commerce.

Let both sides unite to heed in all corners of the earth the command of Isaiah — to "undo the heavy burdens -. and to let the oppressed go free."

And if a beachhead of cooperation may push back the jungle of suspicion, let both sides join in creating a new endeavor, not a new balance of power, but a new world of law, where the strong are just and the weak secure and the peace preserved.

All this will not be finished in the first 100 days. Nor will it be finished in the first 1,000 days, nor in the life of this Administration, nor even perhaps in our lifetime on this planet. But let us begin.

In your hands, my fellow citizens, more than in mine, will rest the final success or failure of our course. Since this country was founded, each generation of

Americans has been summoned to give testimony to its national loyalty. The graves of young Americans who answered the call to service surround the globe.

Now the trumpet summons us again — not as a call to bear arms, though arms we need; not as a call to battle, though embattled we are — but a call to bear the burden of a long twilight struggle, year in and year out, "rejoicing in hope, patient in tribulation" — a struggle against the common enemies of man: tyranny, poverty, disease, and war itself.

Can we forge against these enemies a grand and global alliance, North and South, East and West, that can assure a more fruitful life for all mankind? Will you join in that historic effort?

In the long history of the world, only a few generations have been granted the role of defending freedom in its hour of maximum danger. I do not shank from this responsibility — I welcome it. I

> *do not believe that any of us*
> *would exchange places with any*
> *other people or any other*
> *generation. The energy, the faith,*
> *the devotion which we bring to*
> *this endeavor will light our*
> *country and all who serve it — and*
> *the glow from that fire can truly*
> *light the world.*
>
> *And so, my fellow Americans: ask*
> *not what your country can do for*
> *you — ask what you can do for your*
> *country.*

This by true means is the most remarkable part of President Kennedy's inauguration speech. This is what our country fails to live by today. This where our citizens of our great country fall short. Instead of realizing what we can do to make things better, we in turn expect. I live it, I see it, and I experience it in my daily life. Parents expect that their son/daughter receive a quality education, which I agree with, however they are also quick to judge regarding their son/daughter's work. This is an entirely different topic all together, but "No Child Left Behind" is a vantage point that is ruining our children's education.

> ***My fellow citizens of the world: ask not what America will do for you, but what together we can do for the freedom of man.***
>
> ***Finally, whether you are citizens of America or citizens of the world, ask of us the same high standards of strength and sacrifice which we ask of you. With a good conscience our only sure reward, with history the final judge of our deeds, let us go forth to lead the land we love, asking His blessing and His help, but knowing that here on earth God's work must truly be our own.***

The great silver spoon that is put

in the mouths of the public can be good
for a population and bad depending on
where you rate on the pendulum that is
our social class system. Volunteering
to make your country, state, or
community better than it was before
should be a priority of us all.

Chapter 3: Baby-boomer, Generation X, and the Millennial

When did people become so sensitive? During World War II American's were more concerned with spreading values and principles. People knew their neighbors, and better yet helped those that needed it. There were instances where American's seemed interested in their role within the government. Where has this gone and will participation in our great democracy ever return? I call upon those running for the highest office in the land to explain to us, how so much change has led us to near destruction.

The Baby-boomer generation is the

large population growth after World War
II. Many can associate this generation
as a higher achieving and hard working
facet. I found it interesting when
researching this era that there was a
paradigm shift toward the left and not
the right as I had anticipated. I had
no idea that the baby-boomer generation
would give room to generation X and our
country would become more divided. At
this point in our history there was
another dynamic shift back to the
right. It would appear that our
country flirts with both aspects within
the political spectrum.

I am proud to say that I was
raised by a baby-boomer. My parents
taught me many valuable lessons. I can
remember my dad having a talk with me
as a child and saying that I could do

anything that I set my mind to as long as I had the ambition to follow through. That was a very deep conversation and still resonates in my mind today. I do not know if I can say the same for my children, which in turn makes me sad. Experts predict that generations after the baby-boomer age will not experience continued growth economically. Thus, children for the first time as American's will not earn as much as their parents in his/her lifetimes.

Think about that for a moment. Generation X and depending on how it develops, the millennial will not earn as much as their lineage. The American Dream will seem almost unreachable during this time. I would say that in order for us as a nation to bounce

back, we need more work ethic. We need
to roll up our sleeves and work harder,
save more, and attempt to bring back
the American Dream. Possible? At this
point economically speaking, I am not
ready to drink the Kool-Aid. Not
saying that it won't happen, but not
without sacrifice.

Where did all go wrong?
Discipline, education, political
structure, business practices, and
other varying topics can be looked at,
through various research studies.

However, if we as a nation are too
consumed or lazy, these studies are
worthless. If we are not grounded and
ready to sacrifice even a little bit?
There can be no improvements made.
Letting go of ego would be a rather

foundational approach to this matter. Can we really blame Generation X or do we blame the current generation for our wrong doings? I would say it is a mix of things that took our great country towards the spiral of doom and gloom. There I said it. Many of my former students have listened over and over to Dr. Doom and Gloom in the classroom. It is time to rise up and take our country back and to not be so sensitive during the process. Operation Butt-hurt is about to set sail and we all need to make sure we are ready for what could take place if we do not improve our American Dream.

Generation X is the generation that was born to the Baby-boomer generation. We were able to learn from our predecessors and their habits and their longing or a more progressive and liberal outlook on life, liberty, and the pursuit of happiness. Thus the WIFM. What's in It For Me! We have shifted from J.F.K's speech during this generation. We all seem to be looking for what we can get instead of the what we can make concepts. During this generation, which is the post-Vietnam War era, we started taking many things for granted. We were also about to embark on the largest technological advances in the history of the world. Were we ready for it? We certainly acted the part.

The Baby-boomers were not afraid to show love as well as wrath when it came to discipline. Often times we are put in situations where discipline is needed in order for our children to understand the ramifications of their actions as children. If we choose the rod we should always show love and compassion before doing so, much like the baby-boomer generation.

The millennial generation are those that are considered to be the offspring to generation X. Both generations strive to better themselves in many regards, but both seemed to be more reserved when it comes to what interactions are preserved. When looking back at my upbringing there were many great lessons learned through consequence. Has this shifted for today's youth? This is a great question that we will ponder as we go through the technological age of our development or demise depending on who is talking.

Chapter 4:   The Wooden Spoon

In today's day and age when discussing punishment, there are a broad range of emotions that come into play. In our household, we raised our children to respect adults, ask for permission, stand up for your beliefs, play nice, and say thank you. When my children act up, they get punished. Punished not the way I was punished as a child, but punished like many punish today. You are grounded from all of your technology. It would appear that when I force my child to spend time with me after they have been punished, that they adhere to the rules. This sounds peculiar to say the least.

When I got in trouble as a teen my parents sent me to my bedroom to think about the behavior and the situation that put me there. I was ok with that, as I had a VCR, a Sony Walkman, and a Nintendo. I could now spend time all to myself and focus on what I loved to do; play games. My parents eventually understood the game and took all my technology out of the bedroom and forced me to work off the behavior. There was a catch. As soon as my mother or father returned home from work, they sat me down and discussed the situation. Most of the time it was a heavy-handed punishment that would take place even though I thought I might get away from it.

As a younger version, when in trouble, I can remember the wooden spoon. I remember that wooden spoon vividly to this day. When I would get into trouble and thought that I may get spanked, this didn't bother me all that much because the hand didn't hurt all that much. But when my mother brought out the wooden spoon, it sent shivers down my spine.

There was one occasion when my mother was so upset that she broke a wooden spoon over my butt! Afterwards she hugged me and reassured me that this hurt her more than it hurt me. I laugh out loud at this concept as it did hurt pretty badly physically. The idea that it hurts those doing the punishing more didn't resonate until I had my own children many years later. The thing that both my parents did to

soften the blow was to say they loved
me after they punished me.
If this type of situation were to
happen today in much the same manner,
outside agencies would cry abuse. Is
this abuse to punish your children when
they do wrong in order to help create
respectable adults? This is a
difficult question to many that discuss
such situations. In our generation
there would perhaps be a 50/50 split on
what is deemed appropriate handling of
discipline and inappropriate.
Ultimately no matter how we discipline
our children, there has to be a purpose
behind the lesson.

Chapter 5: The Democrat and the Republican

Want to really raise the pressure in a room, or get someone's blood boiling? Bring up politics around the dinner table or anywhere for that matter. The fundamental discrepancies behind the factions of political principalities in our country could make a grown man cry and run in absolute fright.

I can remember as a senior in High School prepping and completing homework in my American Government class and discussions regarding the two-party system in our country. I had two great teachers both of whom were Democrats and were not afraid to share their beliefs with their students. Often, I debated certain topics like abortion, gun rights, and taxes with my instructors from the Republican perspective. At times they appeared almost upset with the fact that I believed the way that I believed on certain topics. I remember a time when the instructor stated, "Why are you a Republican?" I kindly replied; "Because my parents are!" Hmmmmmm this really makes me think today when I have my own students in my American Government class. I always state that

the student should find what party
suits their personal belief systems.

If I were to ask anyone what party
is the best, they would explain to me
why their party is superior to the
other. I enjoy these debates and love
to play devil's advocate with my
students and anyone that likes to delve
into politics in general. However,
most do not see politics from this
derivative. It is more black and white
to the masses of people within our
country. Or they are so disgusted with
our countries leaders that they feel
their opinions do not matter anyway so
why bother.

I find it interesting when my
students take online quizzes or
political party assessments, they find
they have both Democratic and

Republican tendencies. By and large as human beings we do not want to go against our family's beliefs. There are a few that rebel at the first whim and try and do the opposite of their parents, but again this is slim in my experiences.

By definition a Republican is defined as:

"the more conservative of the two major political parties in the US: established around 1854"
(Dictionary.com)

Conservative comes into play when discussing the differences between a Republican and a Democrat. A Conservative is defined as:

"disposed to preserve existing conditions, institutions, etc., or

to restore traditional ones, and to limit change" (Dictionary.com).

One can gather that Republicans and Democrats alike could congregate a similarity regarding remaining traditional in regards to how the government is running, but not so much on social issues.

In class I discuss the Liberal/Conservative Spectrum in class using a frame reference of my body and the body of the classroom as a whole. Interestingly enough when you look at a room that is roughly twenty feet by twenty feet the mere mass of my chest seems insignificant in size. I begin this discussion by exploring the left and the right with my class. I examine the make-up of each party and explain the differences between the two and then denote the left from the right.

When examining the political spectrum the further right towards Conservatism leads to a fanatical approach to governing. When you travel outside the American boundaries to the left towards the Liberal side of the spectrum the same occurs, but more Socially ran Government operated programs lead again to a fanatical frame of reference. By definition a Liberal is defined as:

1. *favorable to progress or reform, as in political or religious affairs.*

2. *(often initial capital letter) noting or pertaining to a political party advocating measures of progressive political reform.*

3. *of, pertaining to, based on, or advocating liberalism, especially the freedom of the individual and*

governmental guarantees of individual rights and liberties.

4. favorable to or in accord with concepts of maximum individual freedom possible, especially as guaranteed by law and secured by governmental protection of civil liberties.

5. favoring or permitting freedom of action, especially with respect to matters of personal belief or expression:
a liberal policy toward dissident artists and writers.
6. of or relating to representational forms of government rather than aristocracies and monarchies.

7. free from prejudice or bigotry; tolerant: a liberal attitude toward foreigners (Dictionary.com).

There is a plethora of actions within the definition of a liberal that are relevant. One can gather that the Liberal couldn't be further from a Conservative regarding social/religious beliefs.

One can gather that both parties have swayed back and forth like a pendulum over the course our history. This makes the process of evaluating a Democrat or a Republican quite difficult, as both parties tend to resonate differently depending on situations that occur over time. In today's world it would appear that the left and the right are properly placed.

Around dinner tables around the country, I can only smile and chuckle with anticipation of what might be said each night. "These guys running our country are idiots!" "We need term limits for those rich idiots!" "Why do they get such great health insurance and we can't even afford our own?" What happens at your own dinner table?

Do you talk politics? We don't often at our household, as we are a divided marriage regarding politics. My wife often laughs and says that her vote marks mine off, thus getting rid of the negatives. Funny comment to say the least, it is too bad that more people do not take the action to vote during each election.

10 Differences Between a Democrat and a Republican

With the establishment of a powerful two-party political system in the United States—the Democrats beginning in 1824 and the Republicans beginning in 1854—there are some core differences between the two based on very strong political beliefs.

1 Tax Policy

Both parties favor tax cuts, but each party takes a different view on where those tax cuts should be applied. The Democrats believe there should only be cuts for middle and low income families, but believe they should be higher on corporations and wealthy individuals. The Republicans believe there should be tax cuts for everyone, both corporations and people of all income levels.

2 Social Issues

One of the differences between democrats and republicans lie in their views towards social issues. The Republicans tend to be conservative on social issues. They tend to oppose gay marriage and promote marriage being between a man and a woman. They also oppose abortion and promote the right of gun ownership. Democrats tend to be more progressive in their views, favoring abortion and gay marriage, but are strongly for strict gun control laws that limit ownership.

3 Labor and Free Trade

Republicans and Democrats have very different ideas when it comes to the business environment. Republicans tend to oppose increases to the minimum wage, citing the need for business to keep costs low so they can prosper and all Americans can have access to products and services. The Democrats favor increasing the minimum wage so that Americans have more money with which to purchase goods. They also favor trade restrictions to protect American jobs while Republicans favor free trade in order to keep costs low for consumers and make businesses more profitable so they can grow.

4 Health Care

Democrats generally prefer a lot of government regulation and oversight of the health care system, including the passage of the Affordable Care Act, because it makes the health care system accessible to everyone. Republicans, who opposed the Affordable Care Act, believe too much government involvement in the industry will drive up costs and have a negative impact on the quality of care that consumers receive.

5 Social Programs

Democrats across the board believe that government should run such social programs as welfare, unemployment benefits, food stamps, and Medicaid that support people in need. They believe more tax dollars should be funneled into these programs. Republicans acknowledge a need for these social programs, but favor less funding and tighter control. Republicans favor supporting private organizations that support people in need.

6 Foreign Policy

When it comes to differences between democrats and republicans, the foreign policy cannot be missed. Each party has had differing stances in relation to foreign policy over the years depending on the situation. Generally speaking, when military involvement may be required, the Democrats favor more targeted strikes and limited use of manpower while Republicans favor a full military effort to displace regimes that are totalitarian and detrimental to their own people and who are threatening others. Both parties typically agree that sending aid to other countries are a good thing, but disagree on the nature of that aid and who should be receiving it.

7 Energy Issues and the Environment

There have always been clashes between the parties on the issues of energy and the environment. Democrats believe in restricting drilling for oil or other avenues of fossil fuels to protect the environment while Republicans favor expanded drilling to produce more energy at a lower cost to consumers. Democrats will push and support with tax dollars alternative energy solutions while the Republicans favor allowing the market to decide which forms of energy are practical.

8 Education

The parties have different views on the education system of the country, but both agree there needs a change. Democrats favor more progressive approaches to education, such as implementing the Common Core System, while Republicans tend to favor more conservative changes such as longer hours and more focused programs. They are also divided on student loans for college, with Democrats favoring giving students more money in the form of loans and grants while Republicans favor promoting the private sector giving loans and not the government.

9 Crime and Capital Punishment

Republicans generally believe in harsher penalties when someone has committed a crime, including for selling illegal drugs. They also generally, favor capital punishment and back a system with many layers to ensure the proper punishment has been meted out. Democrats are more progressive in their views, believing that crimes do not involve violence, such as selling drugs, should have lighter penalties and rehabilitation. They are also against capital punishment in any form.

10 Individual Liberty

Individual liberty has been a sore

subject of late. Political correctness is on the rise and many people believe that people need to be protected against themselves. Democrats have tended toward favoring legislation that restricts some freedoms, including foods we may have access to. Republicans favor personal responsibility, in that individuals should be able to choose for themselves what they do and what they do not do if

it doesn't break existing laws. (Differences Between Republicans and Democrats, n.d).

Find what you stand for and make a difference in the upcoming election and beyond. United we stand.

Chapter 6: Political Issues: We can't discuss that! (Agenda 21 and FEMA)

What if we were to question the government's motives regarding activities that appear to be illegal? What if we were to say Agenda 21 is a ploy to blast America to a despotic state? What if we were to ask about FEMA camps that are popping up all over the United States? These are all intriguing questions that many whom are well-read in what some would say conspiracies and others who say it is fact is penetrating America.

Agenda 21

Agenda 21 has been floating around for years, I would encourage anyone with an interest in America to take a look and research for yourself some the actions taking place in our country today.

"Agenda 21 is the ELITIST plan to control your life demanding you, "do as I say, not as I do". You will be required to give up your individual freedom, your personal property and redistribute your wealth. Gone forever will be American exceptionalism, American nationalism. The western way of life will be classified as unsustainable. The ELITISTS will use the government to take your money, exercise more power and to control every aspect of your life. Agenda 21 is not a Democratic or Republican "plan", it reaches across the

aisle. The Elite will call us names and make up lies to try and divide us. They use doublespeak as code to reinforce their lies" (Agenda 21, n.d).

Executive Order 1962

Believe it or not these ideals are not a new idea that has been crafted by our current government. During the 1960's President Kennedy passed many laws concerning American civil liberties pertaining to taking away rights in order to protect the country in the event of a catastrophe like a Nuclear War or other factors that might lead America on the brink of disaster. These were real credible situations that could have placed American Citizens on the brink of losing their rights in accordance to the United States Constitution. This was not titled Agenda 21, but was labeled as executive orders in according to FEMA.

"On February 16, 1962, President John Kennedy signed several Executive Orders which would allegedly give certain dictatorial powers to appointed bureaucrats in the event a "National Emergency" should be declared by the President — whichever president is sitting in office at the designated time. At the president's discretion "in any time of increased international tension or economic or financial crisis", the E.O.'s could theoretically be enacted" (The FEMA List, n.d).

It is not my wish to cause great panic to the American public, but only to share information with the country. There are many aspects of these executive orders that are unsettling. For example, if the country were to falter into a "national emergency" as the legislation details, the country

for all practical circumstances would
be put in a lock down with curfews
which in many ways go against the
Constitution.

*. Executive Order #10995: Seizure of
all communications media in the
United States.*
*• Executive Order #10997: Seizure of
all electric power fuels and
minerals, public and private.*

*• Executive Order #10999: Seizure of
all means of transportation,
including personal cars, trucks or
vehicles of any kind and total
control of highways, seaports and
waterways.*

*• Executive Order #11000: Seizure of
all American people for work
forces under federal supervision
including the splitting of
families if the government finds
it necessary.*

*• Executive Order #11001: Seizure of
all health, education and welfare
facilities, public and private.*

• *Executive Order #11002: Empowered the postmaster general to register all men, women and children in the U.S.*

• *Executive Order #11003: Seizure of all airports and aircraft.*

• *Executive Order #11004: Seizure of all housing and finance authorities to establish Forced Relocation Designated areas to be abandoned as "unsafe."*

• *Executive Order #11005: Seizure of all railroads, inland waterways and storage facilities, public and private.*

• *Executive Order #12919: Signs June 3, 1994, by President Clinton. Encompasses all the above executive orders.*

(The FEMA List, n.d).

Granting the government so much power in the event of an emergency of this magnitude goes against who we are and who we stand for. After researching such measures, it draws many outlandish aspirations of a Plutocratic government. I have said this before and I will say it again, Beware of False Flags in order to achieve totalitarianism.

A great friend of mine, author of
"1984 Redux: Say hello to "Big
Brother" Andy Curtiss describes many of
these issues at great lengths within
his book. Andy is a veteran, author,
and MMA fighter who continuously tries
to educate the American people before
it is too late. I was blessed to have
read the book and to have interviewed
Andy on my weekly online radio show.
The following is my review of his book
available on Amazon today:
What a fantastic read. Exceptional use
of research, mixed with personal

aspects regarding the future state of our democracy and governmental make up. This is a must read for all individuals interested in the United States Constitution. There are so many stories of corruption and misdeeds to our fundamental rights. This book brings to light some of those instances. Andy Curtiss is a fine upstanding citizen of the United States and as a retired military man. Come take a glimpse of American Freedom and Democracy at work.

Within the pages of Andy Curtiss' book there are many stories related to civil liberty disgust. Andy was placed on a watch list after he returned from active duty and researched why. The results were staggering to say the least.

Jesse Ventura mentions these issues at great lengths within his past television series and on his weekly radio show. The frightening thing regarding FEMA and Agenda 21 is that it appears that those who would be deemed as a threat to the American Government are placed on a list and watched. Does this circumvent the Constitution? My belief is it absolutely does. Why spy on American veterans and the American people whom all want to make this nation great again. Another staggering find was that those that bring up the Constitution or Constitutionalists are often placed on these so-called lists as well.

Are we Democrats, Republicans, Constitutionalists, or Americans? I would say that we are a nation that has lost its principles and true meaning. We are a lost generation, a nation of naysayers, and uneducated in the means of understanding what our aristocratic elite is trying to promote.

Gerald Banks Appanoose County
Sheriff 1984-2000

Gracie Clark Mrs. Republican

Chapter 7: Politics: It's a Family Tradition

Throughout a large portion of my life, I had political aspirations of running for office to help change America back to what it was meant to be, for the people. Through experience, I am where I belong, a well-read educated man on politics, and

a teacher. I am proud of my heritage.
Politics in my family is a tradition.
My grandfather Ted Clark was an Iowa
State Representative and Senator from
southern Iowa, my father Gerald Banks
was the sheriff of Appanoose County
from 1984-2000, my sister is currently
the elected Recorder of Appanoose
County, and my grandmother Gracie Clark
was nicknamed, "Mrs. Republican".

I had no idea how much power my
grandmother held throughout her
political career. Gracie was the first
female in the state of Iowa to become a
Republican chairperson. Many
presidents and governors met up with my
grandmother to help with their
campaigns in south central Iowa. She
also helped catapult my father's
election bid in 1984 by using her power

to sway political proponents in the area to back my father in his election. As my mother explained it Gracie really knew how to grab her political pundits by the balls and get things done. She would not take no for an answer.

I am about to make a statement that would rock my father and grandmother to the core, God rest their souls, and I am a Democrat and have been one since 2008. Now talk about a Butt Hurt saga to say the least. All is well however, my family understands my stance on politics as I am in education, which many teachers today are Democrats. Make no mistake however I would not vote a straight ticket like my grandmother would have back in her hay day. I vote for the person, their platform, and their background, not the party.

There were a few times when I
would bring up politics with my parents
and grandmother and I would be cut off
at times. There was a running joke
over my dead body would you turn to the
dark side of the force. I laugh today
at this concept but many of my students
in my government class are spitting
images so to say as their parent's
party. I am a Republican, or I am a
Democrat because that is what my parent
believes. There is real life butt
hurt moments when I play devils
advocate on topics such as gun rights,
freedom of speech, and other topics
within the Constitution. Often, I have
to stop the lecture and explain party
politics and party platforms.

I attended a Democratic headquarters meeting in 1991 while a senior in High School. I won't lie to you, I felt as if I had made a deal with the devil, felt divorced from my family, and even felt nauseous at the thought that I was in an arena that my family so deliriously opposed. In 1992 I was not ready to follow my own instincts and voted Republican that year for George HW Bush. He lost the election, but I was able to breathe a sigh of relief within the family.

In my early years as a husband and father I remained a true Republican through and through. When I went back to school in 2002 I changed my mindset and my values. A conversation I had with my brother Joe almost led to a ruined sibling relationship. I mentioned that if I had been drafted during the Vietnam War, I would have wen to Canada. This is a statement that I regret today, but I was only at this time exploring my own political philosophies. I believe we didn't talk for quite some time after this conversation, as he is a devout Republican and a veteran from the Air Force—Chief Master Sargent.

During the 2008 election, I decided I would attend the Democratic Caucus in Appanoose County. Wouldn't that have made Mrs. Republican happy? I enjoyed the Caucus and how the Democratic Party did business. Open and honest and discussions abound in the room. You were either for someone or you were not, this was not hidden like the Republican Party caucus. My candidate did not when; I was hurt but not swayed. My vote did not count for Mr. Richardson, but I did believe in many of his principles. Looking back this is when my political ideologies switched gears. I decided I am an independent, but leaned more towards the Democratic Party.

Chapter 8: 11/13/2015 France Attack and the First Amendment

As I look over social media following the horrifying terror in France on 11/13/2015, it is filled with comments either positive or negative regarding the country in which we reside. We must understand that this is allowed under our fundamental rights as Americans. We should also note that we live in a melting pot society full of many differing ethnicities and religions. Hate is not the answer when

determining the outcome of a truly
negative situation.

*"Congress shall make no law
respecting an establishment of
religion, or prohibiting the free
exercise thereof; or abridging the
freedom of speech, or of the
press; or the right of the people
peaceably to assemble, and to
petition the government for a redress
of grievances"* *(Amendment 1, n.d).*

Make no mistake, I feel for the
people of France and stand behind them
100 percent, however the comments
imploring that our President is evil
and is behind such an event is absolute
malarkey in my opinion. No, I did not
vote for President Obama and no I do
not support many of his programs, but I
do feel that our president did not
knowingly allow such a situation to
occur. Throughout our history, the

United States has always allowed refugees into our country in times of terror and genocide. At no other time in our history other than the Holocaust and the persecution of the Jews have we had an issue of religion as a pinpoint to close our border for protection of our interests. I will expand on my thoughts after sharing some of the Butt Hurt comments, which is protected by the First Amendment.

The following is a list of topics following the attacks on France 11/13/2015

"We should nuke Mecca"

"We can't tell them apart"

"All Muslims are bad"

"It is all Obama's fault, he should resign"

These are pretty exaggerated attempts at trying to defuse such a tense situation, which could lead to a large staggering military engagement with all of the major military powers in the world. In my opinion this is what ISIS wants, a global escalation of chaos, which would allow them to infiltrate easier within all countries across the globe. Our first amendment rights guarantee protection for all American citizens. There will be violence enacted on innocent practicing Muslims within the United States much like what happened after 9/11. What I find most alarming about comments made on social media is that if you respond on the other side of the argument you are often met with violence and harassment. Note I say we live in the Great Butt Hurt generation. The only way I can describe it is like this; suppose you always make fun of others through jokes

and the like and finally when the
others do the same to you and you are
immediately distraught and upset. You
loved poking fun and being the
comedian, but when the joke was on you,
you immediately resisted and were
upset, much like a child that did not
get their way. You my friend are one
of the great Butt Hurt instigators.

Should Americans and those around
the world be protected from ISIS and
other threats? Absolutely. Should we
protect those who need help? I say
this with a heavy heart as my oldest
daughter is serving our great country
in the United States Army. Yes. We
should protect those who need help,
those who are suffering, but only if we
can afford to do so, and only if our
interests in the world call for it and

for no other reasons. At no point can the help given be financially motivated for the plutocratic elitists that seem to run our country.

Thank goodness for the United States Constitution as without it, we would live in a tyrannical world ruled much in the same as other autocratic demigods that have historically ruled our world. I do however state the following not to scare our citizens, nor to say that it will happen, but only as a warning for American citizens.

"The jaws of power are always open to devour, and her arm is always stretched out, if possible, to destroy the freedom of thinking, speaking, and writing."
--John Adams

"Every step we take towards making the State our Caretaker of our lives, by that much we move toward making the State our Master."
--Dwight D. Eisenhower

"America will never be destroyed from the outside. If we falter and lose our freedoms, it will be because we destroyed ourselves."
--Abraham Lincoln

I understand I might sound like a broken record, but please use your inalienable rights and speak out against tyranny that is spreading in our great country. Use your voice, state your opinions, and be well read of what is going on in your world. Also, be kind to each other no matter race, social context, nor religion.

Love one another fruitfully. Also beware of false flags, which can in turn lead to tyranny and your loss of individual rights and freedom.

Chapter 9: Religion? Who said that?

My experiences within the realm of organized religion, is very broad and at times very painful. Religion much like politics is hard to discuss with your peers, family, and friends, especially if you do not believe in the same beliefs. The following story is when I was enamored in religion, I loved it, I longed for it, and I needed it. I would guess no other item in our lives could leave a group or person more Butt Hurt than that of your personal beliefs about religion.

Early Life-High School

I was born to a middle class

family in southern Iowa in 1972. I was baptized in the Episcopal faith and eventually took classes and became an altar boy within the Episcopal faith around 12 years of age. My parents didn't go to church every Sunday but did attend enough for me to learn many of the churches creeds and organized symbology. When Father Jeff Liddy left the area, I never attended the Episcopal Church again until more recently.

After this time period, I really didn't attend church unless it was periodically with some of my friends that I ran around with. When I was fifteen I started attending a Baptist church in my hometown and was immediately struck by the procedures of the church. I felt at home immediately. One Sunday morning, I felt the call to the alter, I felt as if I almost floated to the front of the church that day and felt a very profound feeling that I should become a preacher within the Baptist faith.

Over the course of the next year or so I went to church every time it was available three times a week. One afternoon after services dome of the deacons of the church were talking about basketball and were saying things like that bastard and nigger. This shook me to the core and I never returned to this church again. I became lost again this time going to multiple other churches looking for an organization that I related with to no avail.

As a Parent and a Loving Husband

My wife and I were married in a small Christian Church and went to church often but not as much as we would have liked. Our lives became busy and God was only in our lives at home as we continued to pray together. One afternoon a local church was going door to door and invited us to church. We went and could not have been happier with our decision.

For the most part we felt at home in this little church. Bible at its word was implicated every Sunday full of prayer and hymns. There were also several sermons regarding Fire and Brimstone. One night we went to the church in the early evening hours to pray and rejoice with the Lord. The preacher mentioned the great undoing of our generation and a renewed need for spiritual growth and knowledge of the bible. What seemed interesting about this sermon was that it was happening at the same time that a local paranormal group was trying to make contact within the local cemetery located just outside of the churches doors. I will discuss this cemetery later on, in the book in more detail. Would you believe that my mind was racing with anticipation of what they we're finding out in the cemetery that night?

I was really growing spiritually during this time in our lives. I can't explain the feeling that would come over me each time I went to church, I was almost addicted to the feeling that I would get each and every time we would go to church. We even started

going three times a week at one point.
Is this an addiction, or is it God
taking me by the hand and sharing the
knowledge of the unknown with
excitement and vigor? So many times, in
my life, I have become charged with the
power of the unknown.

We attended church until I found
out our pastor had demonized my sister
at her place of work. He and some
other pastors of the area vilified and
indicated that my sister should quit
her job or she was going to hell. My
sister was doing her job of recording
same sex marriages in our county. This
was entirely unjust in my opinion. If
we are all sinners as indicated in the
Bible and need to be saved by Jesus,
then how can we chastise others for
there undoing? Personally, the action

of judging others based on their place
of work, or their actions goes against
what Christ the person was trying to do
during his service to the world. What
would Christ think of those preachers
that day, as they perceived to be the
judge and jury of a soul of another
person? Personally, God wants us all to
do the very best we can and to treat
others as they would want to be
treated.

Back to the situation, my sister
was doing her job, earning her
paycheck, and doing what our state
government had made law. For those
that know my sister, they know that she
is a caring, loving mother,
grandmother, wife, sibling, and
daughter. She is the embodiment of
what you would describe as a person of

faith and love. Situations like this
bog my mind with questions. How can
men of faith judge so harshly? Was
this a sign from God that it was time
for my family and I to leave the
church? Only God knows. I do know as
a man of faith that God is there for us
when we need him.

How could a man of God act in such
a manner? This experience still
resonates with me today. We stopped
attending church all together after
this situation. I think this was a
test from God. I will bespeak that my
family and I do pray and read the
Bible, but do not attend a place of
worship. My goal is to become grounded
within a religious establishment that
shares my love and adoration for all.
A few weeks after this incident I

attended a coaches convention with my fellow football coaches. We spent time in clinics to brush up on our offense and defense for the upcoming season. The first night of the clinic, we had the opportunity to eat and drink free at a local establishment. I partook and scanned the room, so many coaches doing what I was doing that evening. In my mind I collected my thoughts and contemplated of the book "23 Minutes in Hell" written by Bill Wiese. I don't know if it was the heat of the moment or a figment of my imagination, but I could hear a million screams of people falling in the bottomless pit. I felt anguish, fear, resentment, and remorse for my actions that night.

Participation in church after this experience ceased for my family and I.

I suppose it was a mix of many things, but there was a loss of trust and relationship within our ministry. I will say that there was a long period of time that my wife and I stopped praying together. I deeply regret this time period in our lives. However, we all look at certain times in our lives and realize that we are all learning together. Where the future takes us? This is the true question of faith and spiritualism in my opinion.

Current

We have yet to find a church that we feel comfortable with. We are apprehensive, as virtually every church we have attended has ended very poorly. I do trust God and eventually if we are to attend organized religion again, only God will know for sure.

Personally, I am very spiritual maybe even more than I was when I attended church so often.

I find it interesting that Christians chastise other Christian denominations and other forms of religion around the world. I would say judge not others. I am sure some are raging as they read that statement. It is one of those components I am right and you are wrong, this is what is wrong with America or the world for that matter.

Butt Hurt Syndrome

Ever skip over some of the Christian, Buddhist, Muslim, or other spiritual information on social media? I do quite often, not because I am ashamed of whom I am, but ashamed of

the society we have to live within.
Constantly judging others for what they
say or do. Social Media is like a
small community on steroids everyone
seems to know the truth and you are
always wrong!

I have even shared a spiritual
quote from Islam before and have been
chastised for doing so and this isn't
even my faith. On the other hand, I
have made statements regarding Islam
and have caught grief from some of the
same people that attacked me for my
other shares or quotes on social media.
I learned a long time ago that you
couldn't win. I laugh at such
situations today. People can just be
Butt Hurt and move on.

Ultimately, we must work together,

to stop violence towards other religious institutions and groups. We all need to learn from past history in order to not suffer the same fate that sealed the Holocaust, the Great Native American Undoing, and ISIS type movements from killing innocent human beings. Humanity should be our first and only goal. I hear all the time how this group or that group needs to burn in hell or be wiped off the face of the earth. Will this help anything?

Chapter 10: Confederate Flag, Star Bucks, and a few other Aspects that waste Our Time….

What a way to make the Butt Hurt saga more complete. Discussing the Confederate flag, the situation regarding Star Bucks, and the Ten Commandments. Under the Constitution we should be protected based on our beliefs and speech. It would appear as more and more groups lock on to one another that our freedoms are being detracted from our point of reference.

The Confederate Flag issue that has created more malice and discontent in our racial relations within the United States over the past few months

is staggering. The intent here appears
very clear. The Butt Hurt only rises
when there is something to add fuel to
an already open flame.

Our nation seems to be going
backward regarding instances of race
and a push for civil rights for
protected groups. When will America
wake up and realize what being an
American is all about; being an
American and not a segregationist
society hooked on creating pain and
agony.

I'm sorry but when police
officer pulls you over or asks you to
stop, you need to abide by those rules.
If a teacher tells you to calm down in
the classroom and act appropriately, do
it. When a parent asks their child to

quit acting in a certain way, then by all means do it. We need to focus on the ultimate criteria of the whole scenario that plays itself out.

On and on again I hear our society bitch and complain about how the police use brutality or treat civilians wrongly. One kind lesson that I learned growing up in a great household was that you do what you are told to do and not question. I am sure many of you out there rage when your own child says, "Why?" If someone questions all factors related to the leaders in charge, there is ultimately limited or no respect garnered towards that individual.

I firmly believe had a white police officer not shot and killed an

African American male in St. Louis or in other parts of the world, the Confederate Flag issue would be null and void. People were up in arms over taking down the Confederate flag. They used the race card even without understanding what the Confederate flag meant to all races in our nation. There were folks that fought liked rabid dogs on social media over the crisis. Be careful of the "False Flags" that fly in the chaotic sky each and every day. When these issues were taking place, our lawmakers or the wealthy elitists, the Plutocrats were making legislation that may or may not be positive for our great nation.

Star Bucks decides to change their log on their coffee mugs and boom everyone was up in arms over the issue.

In America we use the Capitalist society, ownership of business is private with limited governmental intervention. If a company wants to do something, then they should be able to do so without a constant fight.

How many of us understand that the great atheist fight towards any symbology representative of religion or spirituality should be taken down on their accounts? The Ten Commandments, which are utilized throughout history as one of the staples of law and order in the world, were forced to be taken down in several locations over the past few years. Even in the conservative state of Oklahoma the Oklahoma Supreme Court ruled that the Ten Commandments Monument violated the State Constitution and forced if off their property. Was this due to the issue where Satanists were asking to place their own statue at the same venue?

Gay marriage is another social movement that is taking the nation by storm. People are following their own morals and convictions and being forced to resign or gag themselves regarding issuing licenses and other items. Personally, I feel that this is a state right initiative much like the legalization of marijuana issue in many states today.

"Tenth Amendment - Reserved Powers. Amendment Text | Annotations. The powers not delegated to the United States by the Constitution, nor prohibited by it to the States, are reserved to the States respectively, or to the people.

(U.S. Constitution).

We should leave social issues up to the state and or communities to decide.

Want to view a battle rage around a dinner table, on social media, or in public? Bring up Gay Marriage or Religion. You will not be disappointed by all the Butt Hurt personification from all those engaged in the conversation. Personally, what a person does behind closed doors is their business, yet another Constitutional freedom set out by our great nation. Ultimately what makes a person better than another? It would seem that we are in continuous conflicts with each other on virtually every facet of our daily lives. If a person is straight, gay, bi-sexual, religious, agnostic, atheist, a democrat, a republican, or whatever, does this make them a degenerate human being? No! A person can be that way without all the things that they stand for. What's worse is that our government keeps running idly by why we are emblazoned in technology, constant dehumanizing, and other forms of dogma to take our minds off the aristocracy that continuously is re-elected time and time again because we feel as if we can't make one difference with what is going on in our world.

The task at hand folks is that we need to band together and take our country back, utilize our fundamental rights as citizens, and stop bitching and moaning about what is wrong in the world. We are still the melting-pot

society that was created by our
founding fathers so many years prior.
Can we get past the Butt Hurt mentality
and rise above issues of decadence that
demoralizes our American existence.
Love one another, treat others, as you
would want to be treated, and educate
yourself on what is going on around
you. Get rid of the Butt Hurt Syndrome
that so many of us suffer from.

Chapter 11: Mr. Trump; Iowans are not Stupid!

Donald Trump like many other Presidential candidates are all vying for attention in my own great state of Iowa. The following is a transcript of his last press conference in Iowa where he is currently trailing Ben Carson in the polls.

"Carson's rise over Trump has been the most pronounced in Iowa, where the first votes will be held in 2 1/2 months" (Taylor, 2015).

And as Trump attacked his red-hot rival, he had another question for

the good people of the Hawkeye
State:

"How stupid are the people of
Iowa? How stupid are the people of
the country to believe this crap?"
he exclaimed.

By the end of the speech, he
appeared to have a different idea,
though, floating the idea of
moving to Iowa himself and buying
a farm.

"I've really enjoyed being with
you," Trump said. "It's sad in
many ways because we're talking
about so many negative topics, but
in certain ways it's beautiful.
It's beautiful."

"It's not the first time Trump has
shown exasperation with the state
in which he was once the heavy
front-runner. Last month, he
retweeted a tweet insinuating that
pesticides on corn had caused
voters to go crazy; he blamed the
tweet on an intern" (Taylor,
2015).

Interesting to say the least that a Presidential candidate would fathom such dissidence to the Iowan Population. Iowans take pride in not only being the first caucus in the nation, but also historically being one of the top educational states in the union.

Mr. Trump how stupid are we when we as Iowans did so well within education before the wealthy elitist took charge so many years ago? Ultimately at the beginning stages of the election process, I fell for Mr. Trump's stance on domestic policies. Today I feel differently. Do I feel that an overhaul of the Department of Education at the federal level needs an overhaul? Absolutely. You cannot just go in and change the system overnight.

Does Mr. Trump make sense on many of the matters that he speaks? Yes, but at this point anyone that is an outsider of Washington politics would be a breath of fresh air when it comes to running our country.

The thing that bothers me regarding Trump is his unwillingness to work with others around him to make the nation great. Assuming that he isn't bsing the masses when it comes to Foreign policies with the world, there would be hesitation as to what his ultimate goal would be as President of the United States. But to make statements like Iowans must be stupid because he is trailing in the polls gets to me hook line and sinker. Look to history Mr. Trump. Iowans are far from stupid.

Mr. Trump please look at America,
as it is, a country full of great
people that want to utilize the
American Dream, not the American Pipe-
Dream. What I do love about Mr. Trump
is he speaking directly from his own
mind
and not from outside interest groups.
The good news is, if he does get
elected, our Constitution does have a
Checks and Balances system in place to
keep our great nation from going into
the brink of disaster. Help us that
are struggling to pay off our debt,
help us lead the world again in not
only the economy but in Foreign Policy.
Lead us not into another war that could
possibly trickle us down much like the
demise of the Soviet Union. Let us be
the best again. I say this not just
for Donald Trump, but for any candidate

for that matter that is elected
President of the United States.
Understand this however, not only
are Iowans listening to what is going
on, but American's from sea to shining
sea is watching with conviction.
Please do not call Iowans or any other
American for that matter Stupid again
Mr. Trump, as we are all working to
make our nation great once more. We
all want the elitist, aristocratic, and
plutocratic state to end.

Chapter 12: Election of 2016

The Election of 2016 will be one for the record books. As we see the power candidates gain power and storm back and forth over the next few months, we should all reach out and utilize our Constitutional Rights as citizens. Find your candidate, and make her/him explain their plans. Educate yourself on the facts presented, not just what the liberal or conservative media remarks to be the truth. We all need to understand that just because it showed up on Google on the first few lines, that it might in fact be tainted truth for the benefit of the Aristocratic leaders within our government.

Bernie Sanders, Hillary Clinton, and Martin O'Malley are vying for the Democratic nomination. If you are a Democrat, whom do you most resonate with? I have had the pleasure of corresponding with Bernie Sanders, who appears to be open to all Americans. Hillary is the front-runner in my opinion and is attacked quite often from not only Republicans but from many across the board for not being honest in her dealings as Secretary of State. One thing is for certain; the Clinton's are master politicians and will fight and claw to the end.

Pros

• *Understands Washington Politics*

• *Has a great leadership base behind*

her.

• Foreign policy

*• Domestic policy (Education and
Economic Driven)*

*• Has Bill the Master Politician in
her Arena*

Cons

• Has become a Washington Insider.

• Benghazi baggage.

• Is backed by big business.

• Often switches stances on a whim.

The biggest obstacle that Hillary will face in this election is that it remains to be seen if the American public will take issue with past blunders both foreign and domestically speaking.

Bernie appears to be in a distant second place at this point of the Democratic nomination. Bernie has been noted as being a Socialist on many of his dealings in American government. He does however want to rid American of the elitists that run our country. ***"This great nation and its government belong to all of the people and not a handful of billionaires, their super PACs and their lobbyists, "Sanders remarked (CNN, 2015).***

Bernie appears to be less inclined to punch back in the early stages of the debates. He wants to make America great.

Bernie is currently focusing on the economy, education, and is more domestic policy focused.

Pros

- Economy focused.

- Driven by the people.

- Understands Washington Politics.

- Will fight against Interest Groups.

- Driven to bring back the Middle Class.

Cons

- A known Socialist/Democrat

- Unknown budget speculation.

- Washington Veteran.

- Not backed by the Democratic elite.

- Not backed by the media.

Relatively unknown Martin O'Malley may be the wild card in the race for the White House. O'Malley is more brazen as to go against the Second Amendment as he had done so during his reign as Governor of Maryland. At this juncture, I would say O' Malley will make a push but will fall short behind the other two major Democratic players.

On the Republican side of things we see a massive wave of candidates vying for the top spot. Around my area they are pushing for either Ben Carson or Donald Trump to win the nomination. I would anticipate that this race is far from over as there are many that may rise to the top. Personally, I felt that Jeb Bush would be the greatest threat to the Democrats, but after several debates and polls, it would appear that this is not the case. One thing remains consistent, the Republican presidential race is wide open at this point. I would anticipate that even Marco Rubio could rise up in the coming weeks as one of the contenders. At this point, Trump and Carson have the edge.

If I were to make a prediction at this juncture, I would say that Clinton and Trump would be squaring off in a general election that will be one for the ages. Not because of all the noise that each candidate will make, but the importance of the election on the balance of Homeland Security, Economy, Education, and National Security. Whoever is elected President in 2016 has a tough job. Bringing together a nation of Butt Hurt personified individuals will be difficult to say the least.

Chapter 13: Laying the Ground Work

As I was putting away the laundry, I began contemplating on what is wrong with my life. I am a happily married man; I have three wonderful children, a son in law, and a beautiful grandson. I also have the job of my dreams, a teacher, going to work every day trying to shape the next generation in a country that appears to have gone mad. I am able to ride to work with my wife and children, start my day with great

kids, many of whom come from a very
poor home life, and I get to talk about
what I am most passionate about; Social
Studies. Yes, Social Studies!
Although boring for many and when I say
that I say that from experience as I am
constantly reminded in the classroom by
my students. "Mr. Banks, why do I have
to learn this? I will never use this
shit." Yes, profanity also runs
rampant in our social spheres even in
the comfortably of our own classrooms.
Although I do not condone it, and
redirect, these students need loving
compassionate support that they may not
be getting from home. So why am I
rambling? There is much work to be
done in the United States of America so
the next generation, even my kids, do
not go down the road of the chains that
have been shackled upon myself, due to

many poor financial decisions. I want
to set a mark on society and break the
chains and begin my life again towards
the road of the American Dream.

The American Dream you say? Many
would laugh and scoff as to what it
really is or means. I am going to
share my story, along with many other
experiences of folks that have become
chained and shackled economically in a
system that may not work anymore. This
is a very distasteful way to examine
the American Dream, but in reality,
until we decide to put in place a
system that works, we will continue to
swing the pendulum back and forth until
there is nothing left to live or dream
for.

Yes, I dream for a life of less worry, less anxiety, and less distractions that cause all sorts of social harm. As I write my feelings down from my daily duty of putting away laundry, I too want to live again in this life.

The American Dream: Do as I say…. Not as I have done-The Butt Hurt Saga Volume II.

Chapter 14: The Average Student

My story starts out in a lifetime that feels like has since passed. Growing up in the heartland of Iowa from middle class parents, I felt I had all the answers to life, and could tackle the world. Immediately this would define who I would become in a sense. I graduated with average grades, which I paid little mind or effort. Even when I got a D, it didn't bother me as it does today. I hung out with friends, lived life on the edge, and had a great time indulging in things that I should not have done. If I could go back and change the past, would I?

There are some things I would change but only if I was able to keep the life that I have now with my loving family. I would however have taken a more serious approach financially and educationally in my life. So many things that we do as we are younger come back to haunt us in most cases. Whether that is from getting poor to average grades or going through the hardship of divorce and paying child support at a young age. All of these stories I will get to eventually, as they are equally important in telling my story. My hope is that folks will

read these pages and plan accordingly
and do as I say and not as I have done.

Shortly after returning home from
the Air Force, which in my opinion
really was my first loss in life, as
looking back, I would have stayed in
the service longer. I was offered
early out due to the end of the Persian
Gulf War and for a medical condition
with migraines. This decision still
haunts me today, as I would have stayed
in for the duration if I had known what
was going to take place only a few
years down the road.

The negative of this is I could
have garnered a scholarship to play my
trombone and sing at North Western
University in Missouri, had I decided
not to follow in my brother's footsteps

and join the Air Force. Don't get me
wrong, I love my brother very much and
I am so proud of his service and all of
his accomplishments, however I didn't
follow my heart and follow my dreams.

This would be my first account of
diving into the shackles that life
gives us. I looked at money and health
insurance as a factor and not truly
living life. Living your life and your
story folks is what it is all about,
enjoying life with limited
distractions. Now I realize that even
the best circumstances have struggles,
but I have struggled more by taking the
road more traveled instead of the road
less traveled. Would it have made a
difference? I don't know, but I do
love the corny mention of Robert
Frost's Poem; The Road Less Traveled.

Upon returning home, I began hanging out with my old friends, and getting into old routines. Moving back in with the parents wasn't easy for me and neither was living under the same old rules under my father's roof. I loved my parents beyond anything in life, but I really thought I had all the answers. Every day I am reminded how smart my parents were when they wanted me to live life and be responsible. What I would do to put my arms around my dad one last time. I thought by going to school and getting an education I would be able to be smarter than my parents. Man was I wrong, dead wrong in many facets.

Chapter 15:   Somethings Got To Give

As I predicted back in 2016 Trump and Clinton sparred in the election unlike anything I have seen in this lifetime. We have also witnessed a rise of ambiguity among our nation and the deepest divide since reconstruction. Something has to give, we as a nation must come together in a hurry or our inalienable rights will leave as fast as they came to us from our founding fathers.

Viewed something pretty disturbing on TMZ today. Was a group of young students making fun of a Native

American Vietnam Veteran doing what the 1st Amendment says he can do peacefully assemble singing in his Native American way. They made fun of him and tried to intimidate.

I do not normally get political, but at this juncture I feel it is time we work together to create a great nation again. We need to dispel the hate and rhetoric that takes place. I have seen a great disturbance over the past few years. Our society has become desensitized to hate, violence, rhetoric, and perverseness that assembles itself in our daily lives. Although desensitized to so much, we have become an overly sensitive country. My hope is that we turn away the hate and assemble together as the melting pot that we are in our nation.

"We become not a melting pot but a beautiful mosaic. Different people, different beliefs, different yearnings, different hopes, different dreams. "
Jimmy Carter

In order to get past hate, we must truly learn to communicate again and lead by a positive example. My hope is that we will learn from our past transgressions and mistakes so history will not repeat itself again.

Chapter 16: Butt Hurt Hall of Fame

The Butt Hurt Saga will continue beyond this first book, giving a true take on America and its people. The ability to understand the issues that take place with us on a daily basis is as important as hugging your children before they go to bed at night.

In order for America to be great again, we must look to the past and see what worked best for each generation. We all live in a new time. We are more advanced technologically and we are better read in school. We must however

get back to our roots, know our
neighbors, and roll up our sleeves
and take our great nation back.

As our world continually
becomes more diverse, we need to
pause and reflect before we act in
a manner that would be negative
towards the growth of us both
individually and as a society.
The Butt Hurt Syndrome needs to
stop. Think before you act and
treat others' as you would like to be
treated.

The Second Annual Butt Hurt

Hall of Fame Topics:

- ISIS
- Religion
- Politics

- False Flags
- FEMA
- Confederate Flag
- Star Bucks
- Donald Trump

References

Agenda21Today. (n.d.). Retrieved November 14, 2015, from http://americanfreedomwatchradio.com/

CNN, "Bernie Sanders takes aim at Wall Street in presidential launch," May 26, 2015.

Constitution of the United States - We the People. (n.d.). Retrieved November 9, 2014, from http://constitutionus.com/

Differences Between Democrats and Republicans. (n.d.). Retrieved November 14, 2015, from

http://www.enkivillage.com/differences-between-democrats-andrepublicans.html

Light, J. (2014, August 14). A Study in
Plutocracy: Rich Americans Wield
Political Influence, the Rest of
Us Don't | BillMoyers.com.
Retrieved November 9, 2014, from
http://billmoyers.com/2014/08/14/a
-study-in-plutocracy-richamericans-
wield-politicalinfluence-
the-rest-of-us-dont/
Plutocracy Retrieved November 9, 2014,
from
http://dictionary.reference.com/br
owse/plutocracy
McDonald, M. (2013, February 11).
Turnout in the 2012 Presidential
Election. Retrieved November 9,
2014, from
http://www.huffingtonpost.com/mich
ael-p-mcdonald/turnout-in-the-

2012-presi_b_2663122.html
(n.d.). Retrieved November 14, 2015,
from
http://dictionary.reference.com/browse/
republican-party

Taylor, J. (2015, November 13). Trump's
Tirade: Comparing Carson To A
Child Molester, 'Stupid' Iowans
And More. Retrieved November 15,
2015, from
http://www.npr.org/2015/11/13/4558
92710/trumps-tirade-comparingcarson-
to-a-child-molester-stupidiowans-
and-more
The FEMA list of Presidential Executive
Orders. (n.d.). Retrieved November

14, 2015, from
http://www.sweetliberty.org/issues
/eo/femalist.htm#.VkeekKJ_Rfg
U.S. Constitution - Amendment 1 - The
U.S. Constitution Online -
USConstitution.net. (n.d.).
Retrieved November 14, 2015, from

http://www.usconstitution.net/xcon
st_Am1.html